On Small Wings

To Jeneatha
a prayerful woman
with a song
in her heart!

Wendy Jean MacLean

On Small Wings

Wendy Jean MacLean

First Edition

A 2021 Don Gutteridge Poetry Award Winner

Wet Ink Books
www.WetInkBooks.com
WetInkBooks@gmail.com

Copyright © 2022 Wet Ink Books
Copyright © 2022 Wendy Jean MacLean

All rights revert to the author. All rights for book, layout and design remain with Wet Ink Books. No part of this book may be reproduced except by a reviewer who may quote brief passages in a review. The use of any part of this publication reproduced, transmitted in any form or by any means, electronic, mechanical, photocopied, recorded or otherwise stored in a retrieval system without prior permission in writing from the publisher or a licence from The Canadian Copyright Licensing Agency (Access Copyright) is prohibited. For an Access Copyright licence, visit: www.accesscopyright.ca or call toll free: 1.800-893-5777.

On Small Wings
by Wendy Jean MacLean

Cover Photograph – Paul Arrowsmith
Cover Model – Maureen Yearsley
Section Art – Wendy Jean MacLean
Cover Design – Richard M. Grove
Layout and Design – Richard M. Grove
Typeset in Garamond
Printed and bound in Canada
Distributed in USA by Ingram,
— to set up an account – 1-800-937-0152

Library and Archives Canada Cataloguing in Publication

Title: On small wings / Wendy Jean MacLean.
Names: MacLean, Wendy Jean, 1955 August 27- author.
Description: Poems.
Identifiers: Canadiana 20220203695 | ISBN 9781989786666 (softcover)
Classification: LCC PS8625.L433 O5 2022 | DDC C811/.6—dc23

To my mother, Arvilla Jean MacLean,
who insisted, as night came and her freedom faded,
"Write this down!"

and to my father, Douglas MacLean
who loves the birds

and to dear Grizwold, our old black dog,
whose love of life was always good company.

On Small Wings

Table of Contents

On Small Wings
- On Small Wings – *p. 3*
- Equinox Scales – *p. 4*
- To Stream Mystery – *p. 5*
- In a Blue Bowl – *p. 6*
- Green Me – *p. 7*
- You Are Continents to Me – *p. 8*
- On a Friday at the Old Port – *p. 9*
- Since I Can No Longer Hear Silence – *p. 10*
- Echoing the Sea – *p. 11*
- Remember the Sleek Skin – *p. 12*
- Never Meant for Flight – *p. 13*
- A Vocabulary for Rocks – *p. 14*
- To Sing the Chants of Fossils – *p. 15*

Yearning For the Song of Robins
- Like Silk Sliding Off a Mountain – *p. 18*
- Caught in a Web – *p. 20*
- Your Bones Get Wise – *p. 21*
- When Your Mind is Clouded – *p. 22*
- In Their Blue Gowns – *p. 23*
- From Your Open Hand – *p. 24*
- Alzheimer Aviary – *p. 25*
- As I Spend the Night Beside You – *p. 26*
- So You Could Sleep – *p. 27*
- Just Come Home – *p. 28*
- Be Gentle as the Night Comes – *p. 29*

Like Ptarmigan Wings
- Across the Battling Centuries – *p. 32*
- Turn Again the Sod – *p. 33*
- The Stories Come Like Tramps – *p. 34*
- She Doesn't Cry – *p. 35*
- With Many Buttons – *p. 36*
- Under the Floors of this Chapel – *p. 37*
- Your Mother Tied Your Braids – *p. 38*
- With Feral Grace – *p. 40*
- Bathsheba From Your Rooftop – *p. 41*
- Rock Hard Words – *p. 42*
- Braiding the Stories – *p. 43*
- The Stone I Carried – *p. 44*

How Sparrows Fall
- Looking For Stones – *p. 46*
- St. Ciaran's Temple, *Inis Mor* – *p. 48*
- The Snow That Does Not Fall – *p. 49*
- Give Me a Word – *p. 50*
- Sophia Watched – *p. 51*
- This Pile of Rubble on Garden Street – *p. 52*
- Growing in Ash – *p. 53*
- One Side Breathes In – *p. 54*
- A Blessing in Angkor Wat – *p. 55*
- Icarus is on the Patio – *p. 56*

Crows' Noise
- In Goose-Feathered Fog – *p. 58*
- Plant Me Here – *p. 59*
- The Waters Find Their Way – *p. 60*
- Lifetime Warranty – *p. 61*
- The House is Up for Sale – *p. 62*
- Thoreau Sells His Cabin – *p. 63*
- Descartes Doubts – *p. 64*
- We Forget the Thousands – *p. 65*
- A Currency of Light – *p. 66*
- These Changing Days – *p. 67*
- Comfort From the Lupins – *p. 68*
- Thousands of Snow Geese – *p. 69*
- Do These Birds Know? – *p. 70*

Heron, Ancient Wisdom
- Three Red Birds – *p. 72*
- The Crows Are Stitching – *p. 73*
- Too Shy to Ask – *p. 74*
- Gabre, Gardener and Gatekeeper – *p. 76*
- Heron, Where You Stand – *p. 77*
- Your Love is Blue and Green – *p. 78*
- To Sit With a Black Dog – *p. 79*
- When the Robins Come – *p. 80*
- To Let the Day End – *p. 81*
- Friends of Ditches – *p. 82*
- The Colour of Earth – *p. 83*

Author Statement – *p. 85*
Acknowledgements – *p. 86*
Author Bio Note – *p. 87*

> *Other echoes inhabit the garden*
> *Quick, said the bird, find them, find them,*
> *Round the corner. Through the first gate*
> *into our first world.*
> T.S. Eliot. "Burnt Norton"

Over these many months of COVID isolation, my experience of live entertainment has been watching the birds in our backyard. They squabble at the feeder, and compete with the squirrels, with drama that gives me language for translating the experiences of community, family and mortality into feathers and flight and nesting.

My father is a great bird watcher. "Look-- up in that tree." he would say, pointing at a forest. He could identify each flash, each crest, each winged friend, from a distance. I am short-sighted and awkward with binoculars, but he passed on his love and delight in the wonder and diversity of nature.

Over the years I have accompanied many people in those last days of their final migration. The honour and blessing of these experiences are at the heart of many of these poems. In the thresholds, on the edges, we meet each other in the mystery, with our wings folded, ready for flight.

Writing poetry is a lot like birdwatching. Words and images flirt and flutter, or hide in the shrubbery with lots of jargon and rhetoric, until I get out my journal and write. Sometimes they soar. As I accompanied my mother in the last year of her life, as her world was changing, and her thoughts were blurring, she kept telling me, "Write this down." I drew strength from the birds, as they went on with their lives, as if the world was not being shaken on its foundations. These winged creatures have provided me with insight into the strange migrations of life and death, and the echoes "round the corner".

On Small Wings

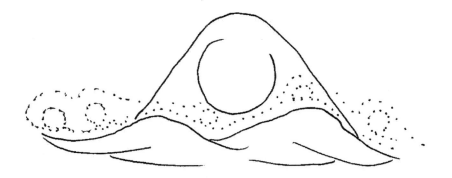

On Small Wings

Be gentle with this moment.
Feel the brush of its wings
as it circles around you.
Hold out your hand with seeds of hope.
When it comes to you, let it rest.
Be still. Hold this wonder.
Be gentle with this moment.
It has far to go on small wings.

Equinox Scales

In the balance of nature
does this equinox festival
of equal day and night
measure with the same scales
the homeless cold midnight hours
and the luscious length of a lover's kiss?

In the balance of nature
does the red of a sunset
equal the red of a fading rose
or the bloody smear of birth
on the head of an infant?
Is spring rain
equal in its falling on the garden
and its rising in the river?

Ask the wild ones. They will tell us
that even the balance is out of balance.
Seek justice, not equality.
Tip the scales with kindness
to give weight to our conviction
that love always asks more of us
because there is no equality
embedded in nature, only grace,
which is without measure
shared in abundant blessing
in the red of sky
the waters of birth
the love of neighbour
and the promise of a new day.

To Stream Mystery

To stream mystery, the composer listens
for the echo of the monks' quills
illuminating the manuscript
of heavens, with the ink of roiling seas
chanting on the shore.
The parchment is stained with notes
transcribing planets for a cosmic lover.

To navigate the planets, and the noise
of thought orbiting this fragile universe
like brushstrokes on mulberry paper
the artist watches
as the composer consorts with Venus
and the violin turns hands to Mercury
and bows to Mars.

Words cannot convey this ache of colour
challenging the gospel with data
collected from stars.
The smallest sound is still a ghost
on the screen, and I watch with my ears
still tuned to read the body
and the planets that revolve
around a baton and a universe
playing together.

In a Blue Bowl

*The curvature of space is...reflected in that psychic curve
whereby the entire universe reflects back on itself
in human intelligence.* Thomas Berry. Dream of the Earth.

In these curved promises of return
a million expectations lie
with winter's worn losses
and summer's faded grace, all waiting
for the glaciers to melt
and the seals to come home.
The ancient prophecies orbit overhead
while in the garden, the tendrils and vines
struggle to hold walls and stakes
so their fruit is not devoured
by rogue denial.
This is the day of reckoning.
The peas are harvested and shelled.
At the table, the planets align perfectly,
pods and gods
in a blue bowl.

Green Me

Green me in this saturation
of spring rain.
Unfold yourself into this day.
Un-pleat my soul.
Dredge the dreary troughs of ego
where judgement lingers
leaving calcified clichés on fumbling walls
I wish weren't there

The trees laugh at me
surfeited by my vocabulary
when all they need
is rain
to open
to splendour
on this May morning

You Are Continents to Me
for Michel

You are continents to me
French valleys and rugged shores
seismic thrusts and tectonic shouts
islands that separate delicate biomes

We find a new world
from the porch
a kingdom from the garden swing
a universe of raindrops and tulip bulbs
and the dog sleeping on our bed
waiting for breakfast
and to be let out

I am not yours to be conquered
you are not mine to be found
I will show you the paths through the forest
as you teach me the ways of the stars

On a Friday at the Old Port

On a Friday in the Old Port
dozens of schools come touring.
Pods of children cling to teachers' ropes
to keep from straying
from stern command and watchful eye.
Caregivers push strollers with ten children at a time
peering out at all the action.

At the IMAX theatre, the children are enchanted
as the 3D galaxy fills the darkened space with stars.
A thousand tiny hands reach out to touch them
and gasp as their fingers fold around nothing
but space.
Dust and light take us to the beginning: a cosmic nursery
for the infant universe.
The children are at home here in this daycare for stars
that hold onto ropes of dust
when time starts to wander and stray too far from eternity.
Children know all about squashed space
and how time expands
as they wait for a snack.
Hubble imagines a new day
and Einstein predicts strands of gravitational waves
streaming out at the speed of light.
Ask the children about the movement of stars.
They will show you their hands open and close
around nothing but dreams
and a ripple of joy sparkling on a fall day.

Since I Can No Longer Hear Silence

Since I can no longer hear silence
because my ears are full of ringing
I listen for the songs of birds
and winds and rivers.
I resent the arrogance of motors
and the backlash and broken mufflers
as they overpower the sounds of a spring evening
without even noticing how they interrupt
the dialogue of courtship and wonder.

The robins are loud
as they flirt and court across the branches.
The cardinals are raucous
as they call from blocks away.
Do they hear the daffodils
in their yellow, babbling blossom?
I wonder if the scylla
growing in the neighbours' yard
resent the racket?

Since I can no longer hear silence
I have to listen
for opening blooms and falling petals.
Since I can no longer hear silence
the willows echo for me
the softest branch of whispering hope
that my heart hears and my body knows
is a call to rejoice.

Echoing the Sea

Raven, in the sweep of your wings
the tide lifts and falls
in moon-driven swells
and midnight troughs.
When daylight shines
on the dusky gathering
of your breast and tail feathers
you waken the underworld
with loud cries.

I hear you from my bed
and remember the tingling awareness
in my feet. They remember
the dance and the sand
and the songs of cliffs and caves
echoing the sea.

Later I will put water in the bird bath
and watch you splutter
at the indignity
of city birds ignoring
your chthonic nobility
and you will scorn my pretense
when I tell you
I only swim in pools of light.

Remember the Sleek Skin

In dreams I remember the sleek skin and the dark waters
pulling me deeper into my own stories
of pebbled beaches and hidden cairns.
All my life I longed to share the bliss of these stories
and the divinity of rocks and wind meeting at the shore.
Somewhere I would find a shepherd's cottage
with my name on an old book open to the invocations
and prayers for starting fires and milking cows.

The call came in waves and ripples
that penetrated the surface waters and found me
where I lingered in fathomless wonder.
The call was relentless, plump with visions
and words that translated ancient longings
into breath and hunger for more.

I wanted to go deeper, to find the place
where my skin is welcome in karst beds
where sea glass is etched with stories of loving.
But the voice was not from the depths
The voices cried from the shallows
from the shore, from the cottage: *Stash the sleek woman-joy
of glistening, wet temptation, and come.*
I wrestled each limb, each muscle out of the knowing
of embrace and allure until I could be fully available
to the words and proclamation that echo the call.

Now in dreams my stories come begging:
Remember the waters? Remember the rocks?
Remember the nights under the sea
and the songs of fish and coral?
It is time to return to my own skin.
Without it, I can't fathom the distance
and divinity flounders in the shallows.

Never Meant for Flight

Caught in the kelp and rubble of pilgrim bones on the shore.
angel wings are washed up on the beach
rounded by years of being tossed
by the waves.
These wings are not made of feathers
they were never meant for flight.
Each broken flash of gospel
once graced the floors of churches
and welcomed royal feet
as spectacular tiles.
The angels remind us to walk kindly
and justly, even when the way is hard.
The angels will support our tired feet
as they round down our fractured ambition
and wash away our vanity.
The angels set us on a path
and show us how to walk.
We do not need wings
to let our love soar.

A Vocabulary for Rocks

I need a vocabulary for these rocks.
It's not enough to call them grey or white
rounded or sharp.
In school we learned to classify them
into tidy categories: metamorphic
igneous, sedimentary.
The syllables fit well in a child's textbook
but now I hear the fires and breathe the dust
as earth pours out her fury
as she changes.

I want a vocabulary to translate the varicose veins
and pockets of fissile sandstone
in my mother's body
after eras of anger and release.

She answers me: *Leave me to settle*
without all this lusting
for simile and words
to describe evolution.

I hear the gravel in her voice
and know it is metamorphic.

To Sing the Chants of Fossils

Long ago he learned how to read
earth's dictionary of pebbles and shells
and how to sing the chants of fossils.
He has a voice that sounds like morning
crunching on the sandman's leftovers.

He chooses his words carefully
to quarry the wonder.
He hews and shapes them
with a mason's precision
building arch and cathedral
with each sentence and vow.

He is teaching his daughter
the language of love.
They stand in awe on the beach
and he tells her the stories of deep time.
He reads the limestone patriarchs
and echoes their dire warnings
about the changing atmosphere.

She has heard stories like this
from her mother, how each breath
fills her with the ancient wind
that blew light from the stars into her heart.

She wants to know if is this why
we shouldn't buy water in plastic bottles?

Yearning For the Song of Robins

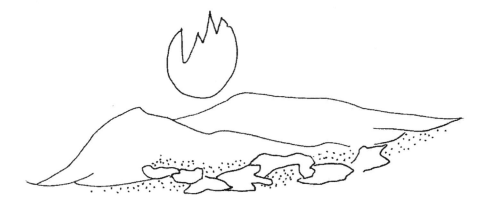

Like Silk Sliding Off a Mountain

There were weeks of days
when memories slipped away
like silk, sliding off a mountain
and words found hiding places
in the wrinkled niches
of your mind

You dressed in stories
spun from spider webs
that held fast to their prey:
the same questions
caught and held, then lost
in the wind
again and again
caught and held
and lost

Remember when you took us
to Alaska to see the glaciers?
We watched them calving
as ancient ice separated from the mother berg
and crashed into the sea.
There is no beauty or joy
in watching these great crashing parts
of your soul, breaking away
from the reality we share
as your world gets smaller and smaller
as the blue midwives carry away
the thoughts that never drew breath
as the melting rivers
round the edges of rocks

more ancient than words
for this kind of love
as Mother Earth labours
to deliver you again
from the sea, from the web
from the mountains
that separate us from you
again and again

Caught in a Web

A sparkle or a mote of dust caught in a web
beckons my imagination,
to investigate the possibility
that I have received a letter from the Divine
out of the Book of Time.
Not a word or a sentence
just a W or a P or an X.

This is only the beginning of a search
for meaning in all the un-swept corners
and unfinished thoughts that call
in strange iridescent whispers
of mornings and wings
and new ways of breathing.

I am afraid to commit
to the adventure
until I have more information.
Why do you correspond with me
in rain and twigs
when I really want a plan?

Eternity, you have all language
all history, all creation
to spell out your demands and delight.
Why do you give me only a moment
of hope in a dusty house?

Your Bones Get Wise

Growing old, your bones get wise.
Your wrinkles tell the truth, with love.
Let them speak like old rivers
flowing freely back to the sea.
See how they ripple across your face
like light, without fear.

When time melts into moments
your heart will shine like winter snow.
Nights are cold and days are long and lonely.
Weather changes us into ice.
Remember how the mountains age?
How winds wear down the valleys?

Death will come, and you can't call
across the hills from night to day,
but at the shore the day breaks open
revealing wisdom's crystal bones
melted into living water
rippling across the divide.

When Your Mind is Clouded

When your mind is clouded
with the dust of memories
granulated and crushed
like pills in jam,
take my hand.
Your skin remembers rain
and mornings when your children needed help
to tie their shoes.

The dust will settle
as it always has
covering you with the prayers of stars
and their little ones
tucked into the arms of Mother Earth.

When your mind is clouded
with weathered words
your heart finds its way back
to the time before time
when light was still waiting
to be born, as dust, as prayer
as love, waiting for children
to tie your shoes.
Take my hand.
Your skin remembers the ties
and laces
and love.

In Their Blue Gowns

Swaddled in blue flannelette,
his tiny arms break free to thrash the air,
catching the light with clenched fistfuls of wonder.
He still sees with the womb ways of knowing
and tastes the residue of heaven in his mother's milk.
Soon this ancient awareness will settle
and he will stop being startled
by every sound that breaks through the strange new day.

Soon he will learn that the blue of sky and the blue of his layette
are separate, and the expanse of time and space
will become just bath-time and bunnies
as the creases and folds of his baby body
stretch into this new adventure.

She is waiting to meet him.
A thousand circles of bubbles and words
wrap her tired body in the perky print
of the hospital gown. She is too tired to care
if the ties are fastened or if her back is exposed.
There is no modesty in this illness
only resignation, and aching to return home.
She is waiting to hold the new baby.

The circle of life begins its return
as heaven draws close
and bare bottoms, creases and folds
expose life's secrets and a new miracle:
unending love wraps them both

From Your Open Hand

At the rippling edge of singularity
dawn pours morning from a pitcher of dust
into your starlit palm, ready to start a new day.
You babble under the covers of your hospital bed
as light draws a brimstone path
across the changing sky.

You are waiting for your meds
to sheer through the pain and wrest your mind free
of the regrets and plans that hover
in the chaos and night.
An imaginary dog keeps you company
in this odd universe of unseen guests
unleashed in these days of awe.

The meds crack open your imagination
and for a brief moment
your eyes regain their sparkle
as you flirt with the stars
in this new constellation of angels and dogs
waiting in the brief lacuna of light
that separates the before and the after
before sending them back to eternity
taking the dog and the dust with them.

The clouds return to your eyes
this time, without the ambition
that long ago turned dust to dreams
as stars whizzed by, taking tomorrow
from your open hand.
As dawn breaks you point to the sky.
You recognize your canine friend
sent from the ancestors
to lead you into the new day.
Sirius keeps you company as you rise.

Alzheimer Aviary

All she ever knew
began to fall away
categories of feelings floundered.
Desire stayed
even as words grew wings
fluttering on her tongue
gaving way to stammering
half sentence, half hope.

Indignant with their infidelity
just a simple conversation
keeps waiting on the tip of her tongue,
languishes, lost, left behind.

Memories, and all moments
now once again, are wee birds,
open mouths, all need and clamour
piercing the silence with body sounds.

Quiet is wordless straw in a nest
reserved for fledglings
starving for sentences and grammar.
Talk is just sky and wind
until the heart begins to babble.

Vultures hover
with vast dictionaries of lost words
xeric volumes of dried-up noise
yearning for the song of a robin or jay,
zealous for a story of a bird who remembers how to fly.

As I Spend the Night Beside You

Nothing can make this chair comfortable
but I pretend to rest
as I spend the night sitting here
beside you
in your hospital bed.
I find comfort being here
when you waken.
"Am I dying?" you ask.
"Not tonight, Mom."

I stretch out my feet
and put them on your bed.
I watch you sleep.
I count your breaths.
I remember
standing beside my babies' cribs
watching them sleep
counting their breaths.

You did the same
when I was newborn
resting in a hospital bassinette
beside your bed.

Tonight we are reminded
of the fear and labour
and the waiting
between the contractions.

I wonder: Did I ask
from the womb:
"Am I born yet?"
And did you answer?
"Not yet, dear."

So You Could Sleep

for Greg S.

The days of vigil
and the nights of waiting
weighed on his tired body
like a million pages
of old calendars.
When the grey light
of his father's dusky hospital room
began to settle
he closed his eyes.
Sleep came and he let go
of the hand he had been holding
so tightly.

He cried when he woke up
and found that his father
had let go too, and moved on
out of the grey
of passing days
and shadowy nights.

You cry because you think
you let him down.
Listen to the wind and rain.
They will reassure you
with breath and tears
that he waited for you to fall asleep
before he unclasped your fingers
and laid them in your lap
so you could sleep
and he could fly.

Just Come Home

Come home anyway.
Do not be deterred
by the sceptres wielding fear.
Do not be delayed
by the dragons that sleep
just at the edge
of possibility.

Just come home.

The same monsters
that are banging at your door
are keeping you prisoner
in your imagination.
They are real
only when you give them power
to deter you
to delay you
to define you.

Just come home
to yourself.
Remember your bold being.
Draw strength
from your soul's willingness
to trust that angels
will get you across
the borders.

Be Gentle as the Night Comes

This raging as night comes
does not slow the darkness.
Anger cannot protect you
when the leaves fall and seasons change.
You have other strengths.
Be fiercely loving
but be gentle
as the night comes
with its own beauty.
You know a thousand lullabies
to ease your soul
past the tired guards
when they try to block the way
from this day into the next.

Let death come as an old friend.
Put out the bridge mix and licorice all sorts.
Be ready to play your cards.
Signal your partner
when you choose the suit.
You have played so many rounds together,
you know each other's moves.
You have friends waiting
to deal the next hand.

This raging as night comes
does not keep you warm.
All the layers that kept you proud
have fallen away.
When you were newborn
your tiny hands grasped at air.
Now in these last days
you can't even grasp
what day it is.
But you still want us to sing.

Like Ptarmigan Wings

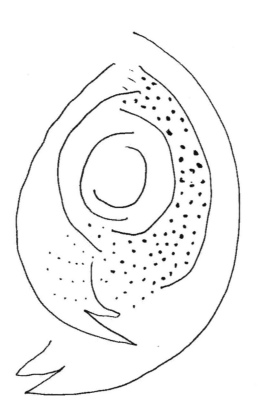

Across the Battling Centuries

The hedgerows and sheep
do not recognize my longing
for roots and relatives

But the stones cry out, they call the dust
from my eyes, the dirt from my nails,
the tangles from my hair.
They make walls that reach
across the battling centuries
to mark the boundaries
that my soul remembers crossing
on the way to the far shore

The tide pulls the ancient child
from my womb out to the rocks,
back to the seals, home
to the ancient rhymes and songs
from the sea to the wind

I hold the day in a rock chalice
carved for a king, as a gift for the child
who welcomes me
across the battling centuries
with his birth cries

Turn Again the Sod

When the stone walls
enclose smaller and smaller spaces,
when the grey crow's call taunts
and the magpie goes looking
for the eyes of the lamb,
Turn again the sod
covering the graves of the un-blest children.

Turn again the words
that welcome the women at the well.
Let the words be a sanctuary
where love is welcome
without unction.

Do not be afraid
when the visits are plenty from the angels
with their hoes and rakes.
They want the souls to grow.
Their prayers are like flowers full of seeds.

Blow, blow, sacred breath.
Blow the seeds past the walls,
that shame the plots of un-named infants.
Blow, blow, sacred breath
send the blessing from God's wild heart
into the graves
so love can grow.

The Stories Come Like Tramps

The grandmothers never spoke
of ecstasy or rapture.
They were afraid
of getting carried away.
They tied their aprons tighter
when memories of bliss
tempted their inner parts
to imagine a different future
and a different past.
The stories come like tramps
to the back door
and call through the screen
to be let in, to be fed,
to be welcomed with tenderness.
The grandmothers turn on the radio
turn up the lights
send the stranger away with a sandwich
before he reveals how he knows them.
Three generations later he comes again,
insinuating himself into my online search
for ancestors. I google him
and search his story
to find out why he loved my grandmothers
and what he left with them
that has my name on it.

She Doesn't Cry

At the edge of my imagination
stands a glimmering possibility,
a light to welcome a traveller in out of the darkness.
I have stirred the ancestors
with my musing and genealogy.
They descend on me in their unfinished mortality
and start a conversation with my soul.
I don't want to listen to these patriarchs boast and brag.
I want to go to the back sheds,
to be with the women as they scrub the blood
out of the white sheets and torn petticoats.
Women will talk to each other
when their hands are busy in hard water.

I want to know about that baby
wrapped in the old blanket in a wooden box
in the shadows. She doesn't cry.
Who is her mother? She doesn't cry.
Will a woman from the house come and take her?
No one will ever mention the day of her birth
or the breasts that nurtured her. She will have coarse, curly hair
but no one will ever say: "You got that from your mother."

The traveller comes in out of the darkness.
Tomorrow he will show me the southern field
where we were conceived, with a silent scream
that we can still hear crying out between the lines
of the genealogy.

With Many Buttons

At dusk, come from your hiding places
and meet me at the fire pit.
There will be many of you
so do not be afraid
that you will be the one with the worst story.

Some of you will argue
and try to thrust your version of the past
onto us, shouting to drown out the voices
of the lost ones who whisper and hum
as they linger by the fire, wondering
if the flames can be contained
when the stories pour out like solvent
and the whispers explode into songs and wailing.

Come from your hiding places
in the shadows and forgotten hedges.
Look how the firelight makes everything dance.

Draw close to the fire.
As you feel the heat warming you, watch
how the night sets us free to be beautiful,
especially in our broken places and tied tongues.
Fear wears a gown with many buttons.
Watch as they open, leaving your soul exposed
in the flickering light.
Watch as dawn dresses you
again, this time in a seamless robe
woven by the ancestors with love
for your baptism, for your new life.

Under the Floors of this Chapel

A hundred years of lies
are hidden under the floors of this chapel.
We ignore them and proceed with our liturgy.
They have been calling
in voices of fireflies
and stinging nettles and elderberries.

Your people fished in the river
and danced at the summer fires
until the hunger days and revival tents
sent you away from the meadows
and the patches of berries
you picked with your grandmothers.

Blackberries still grow in the back hedge
and a graveyard hides the smug secrets
until I notice you in the sanctuary
interrupting my prayers with your honour song
howling in the wind.
The centuries wash over us
splashing in the shimmering light
with truth from a thousand years
of shadows the colour of blood and berries.

Your Mother Tied Your Braids

Your mother tied your braids
tight, to keep them from flying free
across your face.
When you came in from playing
if you had dirt on your face
she would lick her fingers
and wipe it clean.
You hated that smudgy rub
of her hands on your face.
You howled. She laughed.

All mothers care for their young
with their spit and sweat.
Even Earth washed her mountains
with sky spit and the rub of wind
across the face of her beloved.

You are alone now when you howl.
Your tears are polluted like the rivers.
Your face is pocked and bludgeoned
by mines and pipelines
smearing and staining the wrinkles
that long ago were laughter's trace lines
at the corner of your eyes.

Your bones were found
before they were turned back
into mountains.

Beams of radar penetrated the secrets and lies
that were sung at mass.
Kyrie Eleison.
Christe Eleison.

Mother of wild berries and mercy,
Spirit of spring rivers and otters,
Host of sacred fires and ancient stories,
love, healing and hope:
Tie our braids tight.

With Feral Grace

She has a darkness to her,
a raven-sleek mystery
that dares the world
to silence her bold care
for the wild ones.

She learned to be silent
in hopes of avoiding
the noise of fumbling hands
and breaking glass.
Now her home is loud
with the sounds of rescues
and strays who love her
with feral grace.

Trees shelter her at dusk.
She trusts them with her stories.
Thickets and brambles come alive
where she walks.
They know she understands
their growing pains
and their roots spreading at random
in the dark earth.

Life enfolds her
like ptarmigan wings,
white to carry the winter
forest brown to last the summer.
She changes to match the elements
and finds a hiding place
for her treasure:
a soul so rich
that gold has no value.

Bathsheba From Your Rooftop

What kind of light in you triggered the lust
of a king, and his songs, leaving you forever
remembered as a temptress?
Bathsheba, from your rooftop
were you revelling in the sun
as its unconditional radiance
stirred and swelled the air?

After the stone-damp prison
of loneliness in your rooms
you found joy in the touch of warmth
on your skin, and the freedom to see the world
from your rooftop.

Dappled light moves across the stories
in a dalliance with shadows and shame
and sadness, confusing your motives
on that rooftop, with the history of kings and soldiers.

Bathsheba, daughter of a day's silent loss
Will you speak up now, when your sisters cry
and the light exposes the stories?
You too?

The king sent messages and he took her.
She came to him, and he lay with her.
2 Samuel 11:4

Rock Hard Words

Rock hard words
at the edge of an abyss
were not on the itinerary
but we met there anyway

sad and disappointed faces
watched
silenced
holding their breath
in fear
that any gust or sigh
would push us all
over the edge

Did they know
in the end
it was the silence
that had the mean hands?

Braiding the Stories

When the strands and coils
of the helix have been untangled
and the codes have shared their secrets
the three women begin their work
of braiding and overlapping the stories
they never heard
until they found out they were sisters.

The trunk that held silk camisoles
and the first curls of the second child
never told these secrets:
a mother's lies for her son
a Christmas Eve of whispers
the child that was never born.
The regrets and longings were folded
and tucked under the costumes
of superheroes and princesses
whose stories we are proud to tell.

With the passing of the elders
comes a new freedom and a chance
to reclaim childhood and parenthood
and the complicated ties of ancestry.
They have always held the truth in their web.
When the wind blows
the strands still cling to the house
where the stories begin with happily ever after
because they don't dare tell
about that once upon a time.

The Stone I Carried

I carried the stone for days
my hand wrapped around its jagged edges
as if they were baby chicks
and my fingers were the safe wing
of a mother bird.

My hand grew accustomed
to the inconvenience.
I forgot I still held it
until I was needed for a task
that required two hands
and a clear head.

A thousand stones rumbled
from where I had hidden them
in my belly.
They howled and shrieked
until I could no longer ignore them.

They wanted to be held and coddled
and blessed like the stone
I carried
to teach me to let go.

How Sparrows Fall

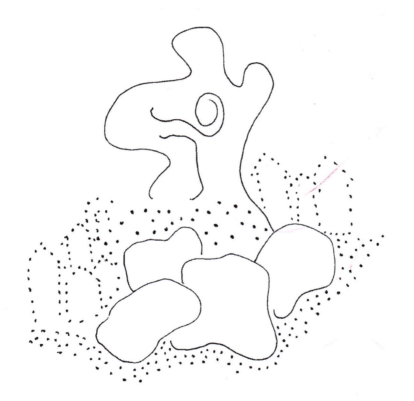

Looking For Stones

The old man never stops looking for stones
that will fit together
into walls
walls into houses
houses into village
village into home

His eyes scan the desert as he watches his goats
goats into herds
herds into market
market into hope
for house
for home

Rocks and hope are strewn across the desert floor
placed by a divine hand
or a star
or a crisis
in the universe

Walls, stones, rocks gathered into lines
to divide, lines to protect
rocks, walls, goats

A desert creation story:
the old man never stops looking for stones
to fit together
into a story
to remember the joy
of a home
and a herd
and a sunset, red with the dust
that was once stone
without fear

Stones fit together
words build the house
earth, clay, rock
one body, one day
one shelter, one home
rocks, goats, house
stone, story, planet

St. Ciaran's Temple, Inis Mor

Squabbling did not round the edges
off the rocks
but the endless nagging
was enough to tonsure the mountain.

The monks gave up
pretending to be devout.
Limpets, lies and lust
were their diet
between the prayers and the pouting.

They stopped coveting the gannet's precision
long ago, preferring butter and beef
to eggs and dried fish.

St. Ciaran led a simple life
so pure, so true
that he had to leave
to build a bigger one
at Clonmacnoise.

The Snow That Does Not Fall

It seems like everything we know and treasure
has been destroyed. There is no peace.
Doves fly like rats in the city skies
and school walls are defaced with hateful symbols.
Does the sun know about the tears
of widows and orphans walking in numb darkness
this shining day? Do the clouds know
about the death of six men at prayer?
Yes, answers the sky, I know.
Yes, answers the day, I know.
The snow that does not fall
makes a prism in the sky.
This is not a rainbow.
This light does not bend or arc.
It is a straight line of coloured light
breaking through the dull resignation
with a new story: winter hopes for a new day.
The flood of tears makes a sign in the sky:
a covenant of faith between neighbours.
The sky's blue grace holds us all.
Our prayers shine in the new day.
Yes, answers the sky, I know.
Yes, answers the day, I know.

Give Me a Word

Give me a word
for this rubble.
String together letters
that spell yellow and red
rags and fuselage
and broken wings.

Give me a word I can read
to make sense of this accident.

Give me a word
that can hold the names
of the martyrs while they pray,
A word that is louder
than the words written on a gun.

Give me a word
with an accent
that is the same in any language.
Give me a word
for shoes
that wait in silence
for the dead
to need them.

Sophia Watched

Sophia watched
as her son raced his trucks
back and forth on the velvet pews.
She knew he needed to explore
the shadowy corners
of melody and prayer
in the sanctuary hushed in vigil.

Some of us held our breath
when he got close to the fire
but he did not linger long by the candles
we had lit with such care
to remember the martyrs.
The child was not afraid
of the inferno of prayers.

He wanted to play, to dance,
to watch us watching him.
Sophia trusted that we would love him
just as she loves him
and that she would love us
for loving him.

The candles burned down.
Our prayers melted into the sand.
Sophia took pictures with her cell phone
to share with the world.

Our vigil cannot end
until all children
can stand in the light
without fear
of prayers catching fire,
until this little boy is free to dance
in his little blue boots
while we sing Hallelujah.

This Pile of Rubble on Garden Street

This pile of rubble on Garden Street
used to be a hospital.
It was sold and dismantled brick by brick, wall by wall.
When the outer layer was torn away
the rooms were exposed like a gaping maw,
an open mouth, a mended wound.
These piles of rocks don't tell the stories
of people healed, babies born,
families gathered around the bed
of a loved one who waits for death.
Long ago the Sisters of Providence built this ministry
of hospitality and hope and healing. After her death
Sister Josephine walked the halls keeping
company with ghosts and angels.
These mountains of concrete remnants
are a promise for a new day
when the space will be used for new hopes
and homes and a new hospitality
in spirit, opening the heart of God.
On Remembrance Day, we remember the rubble
and destruction of cities and homes and people from war.
We remember deaths and families
changed forever by trauma and shock.
Bricked up faces hide the inner layers and silent wounds.
On Remembrance Day, if we don't tell the stories,
if we don't give thanks for the sacrifice, will we remember
why we are standing together
with ghosts and angels?

Growing in Ash

Orange afternoon skies
announce the return
of dust and fire
as if creation is recalling
the rutting and burning
of stars and planets

Particles of forest
sweep across continents
choking us with the same wind
that swept over the void
separating light from darkness

It is not too late to begin again
announces the rain
into the budding panicles
of flowers growing in ash
and rose-coloured teachers
growing in tree trunks.

Australian photographer Murray Lowe, captured the rapid regrowth of flowers in New South Wales, after more than 63,000 hectares were destroyed by wildfires.

One Side Breathes In

At the entrance to the temple
two stone lions keep guard
one breathes in
one breathes out
Light and shadow exist together.

In the garden, the bamboo and cedar
hide the sky
to prepare us
for the opening
from darkness
to light
light in, darkness out.

Life is fragile and fleeting.
The leaves of the Japanese maples
are delicate on this November day.
Life is etched with the elements'
same fine hand.
You are tired from your treatments
and we are too shy to pray out loud
too tender to speak of life and death
so we breathe in and out
light and shadow
and the stone lions keep guard.

A Blessing in Angkor Wat

Just a short distance from the centre
of the universe
(and the stone that marks the place)
the priest sits
dispensing his blessing.
His words —to my ears—
are like the chattering of birds
a singsong language
I do not know
echoing off the temple walls.

They could be prayer
or warning
or this day's babbled news.
I do not know.

I trust his voice
his place on the mat
his incense and flowers.

He slaps my wrist
and ties it with a red cord
binding this moment
to all moments
this temple
to all sacred space.

Once I was bound to my mother
by a cord.
On this snowy morning
far away
my pulse beats against the red strings
with a memory of prayer
and the slap at birth
that reminded me to breathe.

Icarus is on the Patio

Icarus is on the patio trying out different kinds of glue:
mucilage, white glue, super glue.
He likes the super glue. It suits his plans.
He has a motley collection of verbs and feathers
from old books and road kill:
pins and tales and a handful of down.
His father made a frame for wings years ago.
It has been in the shed with the garden tools and mower
waiting for the perfect moment to be finished.

Catherine spends her days in a big chair
at the door of the residence where she waits
to welcome visitors. Mostly, she sleeps,
nodding into old dreams until the door opens
and she wakes up, ready to sparkle, with words shining
like old silver, polished just for company.
Some days she just sits in her room looking out the window,
still waiting for visitors. They come on wings to the birdfeeder:
a sparrow, a triplet of chickadees, a couple of flirting red poles,
jangling, mating and resting briefly in the branches
like old stories, and words that come close, then fly away.

Icarus remembers Catherine and how she taught him
in Sunday School, about sparrows, and how they fall
and how God loves the little birds.
All very well, he thinks, but this is a time for eagles.
This is a time for proclamation! Exegete the skies!
Deconstruct the limitations of naive gusts and billows.
Take the words and FLY!

From her window, Catherine sees an odd bird
rising in the sky on awkward wings.
He is too proud to come to the feeder,
too proud to get comfort from old hymns and stories.
That does not stop Catherine from blessing him
and healing his broken wings with her prayers.

Crows' Noise

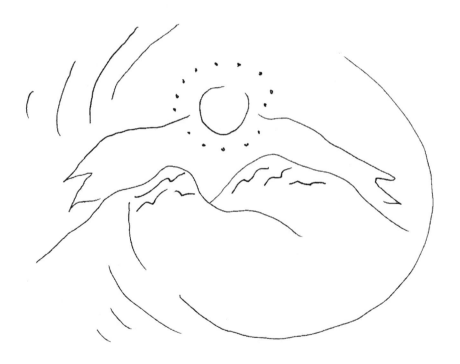

In Goose-Feathered Fog

This grey goose-feathered fog
wraps the day under its wing
gathering thoughts, like chicks,
from their scattered expectations
for a time of contemplation.

In the muffled surrender
to limited sight, I hear
the sounds of freighters on the river
and trains en route to the city
and my own footsteps on the pavement.
They are as loud as light
breaking through the dull skies
with the good news
that even movement is stillness
this morning.

Plant Me Here

I did not choose this ecstasy
slipping her hood over my perception.
I did not choose the seduction
of satin centuries
sleekly wrapping me
in robes of awe.

My face longs for the mist
of clouds awakening my senses
to this moment
as if there is no other.

My feet long for the forest
and the fallen leaves
that hide twigs and branches
that will startle me
when they crack and break
if I don't walk carefully.

I did not choose this ecstasy
of cloud-walking
and shade-foraging.
Plant me here,
in the wet wisdom.
of today's sky
and the geese on the neighbour's pond
in this moment
as if there is no other.

The Waters Find Their Way

From the mountains
the waters find their way, underground
as rivulets and streams of spirit
water the earth from within

I love the movement of water
as it ekes and edges
through the body of this land
I spend my life divining the flow

And now I find the waters I love
have worn away the foundation
of my heart's refuge

Stones no longer meet at corners
nothing holds them to each other
mortar is exhausted by moisture

When the rain comes
I recognize the river
relentless as it falls and flows
into my basement

I turn my face to the sky.
Let this day wash my soul from above.
Leave no trace of the waters
that carved this emptiness then left me dry

Life-Time Warranty

The roofers came with their quotes and boasting
about service and quality
and life-time warranties.
In fifty years
this house will be two hundred and sixteen years old.
The walls will be bragging
about how many coats of paint
hide their wrinkles.
The garden will have suffered
generations of neglect or re-design.
And I will be too old for dancing.

One company assures us
of the quality of their workers.
They tie them to the roof
and come to check, regularly
surprising them, and taking pictures
for evidence.
I hear the house groan
at the invasion of her privacy.
When her struts are exposed
nothing will be straight
especially the promises
in the contract.

The House is Up for Sale

Gradually the walls begin to scorn the emptiness
of the bland, staged intentions of saying nothing.
The house resists being made into a show piece.
It is up for sale, not betrayal.

Take us back, the walls cry
as summer light fades.
The windows ask for mercy
as the house is stained with gold.

This house has contained us for many years
without a word of resentment.
Now the foundation buckles with rumours of loss
and moist gossip intrudes the conversations
of floor and ceiling.

We silenced the house
when we wanted to sell it
but the kitchen insists on scents and spices
from apple jelly and foraged fruit.
They claim our hearth
and rescue the seasons of stone and forest
with stories that we used to tell
when our house was still a home.

Thoreau Sells His Cabin

When the wind blew
through the cracks
of your carefully constructed prose,
and the frost heaved
in the roads, and the branches huffed
at your metaphors,
did you lose heart?
Did your invisible readers
seep their way
up your damp walls
and surround you
with their expectations?
Or did you just live
frog-like in the winter pond
trusting that time would work
the transformation off the page
and you would never have to entertain
endless drafts
and re-writes?

Descartes Doubts

Descartes doubts the reality
of everything
beyond his own existence.
His lonely thinking
ripples through the pond.
A frog breaks through the nothingness
and sees dull eyes
and a heavy body
looking at her through the scum.
"It is all very rational," she explains.
"I jump, therefore, I am."

We Forget the Thousands

With his eyes bulging
above the water
his wart-sleek body
contradicts the awkward slime
and buzz of the swamp
and river stories of waiting.

He waits in the creaturely creases
where transformation enfolds tadpoles
waiting to be changed
when spring comes.

We forget the thousands of siblings
that shared the gelatinous ooze
of his first home.
We forget that once he had a tail
and no voice to punctuate the night
with his story
of what he was, and what we were
in the cosmic soup
our first home
in a universe enfolding
the stories of waiting
to be changed.

A Currency of Light

Everywhere I look, I see gold.
It falls from the skies, a currency of light
a foliage of rapture.

Even the gravel of the road
has pebbles flecked with gold,
nestled into quartz and the grey news of stones
wedded to glaciers.

Everything is on the move, being spent, being saved.
Seasons change. Leaves fall.
I look up, I look down.
The beauty makes me rich.

Everything is on the move.
Seasons change. The trees are bare.
I look up, I look down.
I am rich with fools' gold
that cannot be spent on anything
but joy.

These Changing Days

Like the grey grizzle
of these changing days
I long to fall from the sky
to find myself grounded
in the welcoming earth
of this place, this time.

In the atmosphere
anything is possible.
I have been air
and mist and rain
and moved easily between states
but it is time to leave the clouds and wind
and come home.

The river is still frozen
but crows' noise louder than rain
is announcing the coming days
to waiting trees
and anxious people.

Spring will return and declare
in purple and green broadsheets
I am here
and we will be ready
to welcome her home.

Comfort From the Lupins

When winter comes
with its blue shadows
I will draw comfort
from the lupins
as if they are still blooming.

There is no need for me
to be constrained
by the season.
I will not be there
for the purple skies
and cold nights
to contradict my fantasy.

The past is just as real
as the future
and on the snowy days ahead
I will need flowers
to reassure me
that I haven't forgotten
the freedom of summer
and how you loved me.

Thousands of Snow Geese

Thousands of snow geese
on the open river
ripple the water
and babble in angel song.
Gabriel, with your white wings
and bold flight
do you have news for us?
What promise do you bring
for us to ponder?

The child will come like snow
on a winter day
exquisite and ordinary.
You will recognize him
because you took time
to look
and wait.

Wings and words will pass away
but this moment you will always have.
As the snowflakes melt
remember the snow geese
and the river
all moving, all still
all now
all long ago.

Do These Birds Know?

Do these birds know
it's still winter?
Or have their hollow bones
been seduced by spats of sunlight
masquerading as the long rays
of warmer days?
We expect wisdom from creatures
who do not have to navigate
the gusts and swells of politics.

Their bones ache with animal instinct.
They have not been fooled by the calendar.
Their awkward formations
in overheated skies
in a confused climate
are not a sign of spring.
The rivers never froze this year.
When the robins return in January
will it still be winter?

Heron, Ancient Wisdom

Three Red Birds

In the tree near the hospital
three red birds are jamming
with the grey winter day
cheekily defying the dull skies
with their outrageous imitation
of the colours of dawn

They busk from one tree to another
with bold confidence in their invitation
to make a chorus of the bare branches
for a love song about courtship
and nests to hold little ones

This is winter, not a time for new life
but the three red birds keep calling
brazenly insisting that we take time
to admire them
without wishing it was summer
without wishing
you were here
to sing with them

The Crows Are Stitching

In the far woods
the crows are stitching
patching yesterday to today
hemming and shortening
moment to moment
embroidering the calendar.

They thread their needles
with earth, air, fire and water
as they gossip about eternity.
"God's bride," they laugh.
"Yesterday's serving girl," they squawk.
"Today's joy," answers Wisdom
from the high boughs
of the tree of life.

Too Shy to Ask

If you are too shy to ask
if it is really spring
if these fluttery fancies of friendship
mean more and more and more,
Ask the garden to tell you what it means
to hold the secret underground.
Ask the tulip bulbs you planted
how it feels to push through Spring's cold soil
to grow and grow and grow.

If you are afraid to trust
that summer really comes,
Try embracing long days of adventure
for more and more and more.
Ask the heron to show you how to wait
in shallow waters at the shore.
Ask the cherry trees in blossom
how they trust when skies are full of rain
they'll grow and grow and grow.

If autumn catches your eye
with the flaming glory of changing leaves,
Be ready to sing with maple and birch
and larch and beech.
Ask the forest how to stand naked
with your roots holding you
as your leaves fall to the ground.
Trees know the wisdom of letting go.

If you are so bold to ask
the winter for a kiss
when flirting with shivers and hoping
for more and more and more,
Let the falling snow show you the glory
of each unique flake as it falls.
Taste the frosted breath of wonder
as you pause to hear the world invite you
to grow and grow and grow.

Gabre, Gardener and Gatekeeper

Dear Gabre, gate keeper and gardener
Even in dreams you waken me
with the scratching of your rake
as you clear away the leaves
that fell from the tree in the night
as I slept.
Throughout the day I hear the clang of metal
as you open the gate
to let people in or out of the compound.

In my dream you hold a candle.
Are you inviting me into the garden
or outside the gate?
Maybe you are just showing me
the beauty of both
and clearing away my fears
of leaving
or being swept away.

Heron, Where You Stand

Heron at the edge of the shore,
find us where the day ends.
Meet us in the dusky confusion
where we aren't sure
if we are turning into night
or being transformed
into deeper confidence
in the mystery of unknowing.
Daylight waits patiently
as the seasons turn
as the earth turns
as we turn
to you, where you stand
watching us
watching you, ancient wisdom of threshold places.
We are uneasy trying to balance
these wobbly visions of who we are
and who we are becoming.
We watch you standing in the twilight
and try to make sense of this turning.
Hush our fears as the night deepens.
Give us joy in the mystery of unknowing.
in the shadows
and the reflections of deep time
and the silence of the ancestors
at the edge of this day

Your Love is Blue and Green

Your love is blue and green
cedar spire and cathedral sky
the day growing and sweeping
up to the heavens, down to the soil.

Your love reaches deep and wide.
Your presence flutters on yellow wings
and sentences that fly
from sacred text
to my heart.

Your love is blue and green
sea swept and forest blessed
as seasons change and call
from the summer pond
to my winter prayer.

To Sit With a Black Dog

In my mother's days of wandering between worlds
a black dog sat on her bed
conjured from the realms
of archetypes and ancestors.
She was annoyed
that this canine phantom
would be so bold.

So now it is my turn
to sit with my very real (incontinent) black dog
keeping me company. He is old
and this weather makes his joints ache.
He rests beside me
as I muse and ponder
and go seeking ghosts and meaning
on this rainy morning.
I am glad for his quiet adoration
and his quiet confidence
that I love him too.

But now it is my turn to say goodbye
as my old black dog is called
out of his suffering back to the ancestors,
into the dreamworld.

Today I am lost wandering between worlds
as I long for my mother
and my beloved canine friend.
Someday I hope he will sit on my bed, in spirit
as I move across the threshold
to find my way back to them both.

When the Robins Come

When the robins come in gusts of hope
breaking into the dun leftover of autumn's weeds
we rejoice. I see their red flash of promise and remember you
and your father's fields, waiting to be turned over
for the new growth.
From where you lie you can see the forest at the edge of the field
but you have to imagine the robins.

Your bed is in the room where your father was born.
He hides his tears when he passes you sleeping
just as his mother hid hers as she waited with your grandfather.
He knew the crops would grow without him
but the soil under his nails could never be scrubbed out.
You were afraid to tell your mother about what was growing in you.
You talked about the weather, the grandchildren, the bulbs in the garden.

In these years since you have been gone, I wait
for the robins, and though they could not keep their promise
to you, they persevere each spring
to break through the fallow end of winter days
with a flash that reminds me of you
and your courage as you moved from one season
to another, without seeing the robins.

To Let the Day End

in the Cemetery, St. Kevin's Church, Glendalough

You will always be young
to those who lost you at your death
But earth welcomes your ancient soul
and waits, with a blanket of soil
for your cradle of bones.

Your family keep a candle, lit
on your grave.
In the strong winds
the light moves and dances
as you moved and danced
in those last days.

In the darkness, the flame
keeps vigil, rocking your dreams,
the little ones who gather round
for a story, of how this wind
is the same gusty gift
of breath and spirit
that makes life from death.

The wind never stops whistling.
The wind never stops keening.
Song and dirge mimic
ancient soul, infant grace.

In the darkness your spirit is close.
I recognize you in the lamb's calls
and the way the mothers wait
for their little ones to nuzzle and rest
safely content to let the wind blow
to let the light flicker
to let the day end.

Friends of Ditches

When I walk past my garden
the scent of milkweed
invites me to marvel
at how this disorderly patch
of determined perennials
has been transformed
into an apothecary.
These are healing plants.
In the plant catalog they were called
Asclepius, named for the god of medicine.
What a surprise to find these friends
of ditches and meadows
healing me with dreams of butterflies
and the visits of Psyche, the soul,
in her migration.
In the fall the milkweed pods will open
like a book of memories.
Spirit-led and free
and in confidence of life planted
and blessed, they will be scattered and blown
till they rest in the body of Mother Earth
holding in prayer the new generation
and their dreams of butterflies.

The Colour of Earth

Let this prayer be twilight or early dawn.
These are changing times, blushing, naive.
Dawn is confident enough
not to worry about what lies ahead.
Twilight is drenched in gratitude
as she lets everything go.
They take turns praying for beginnings and endings.
They hint in shades of red or gold
anticipating glory, remembering cloud.
In these times of opening and closing,
meet me in the twin shadows
of everything and nothing.
Rest with me in the silent shining
of darkness the colour of earth.

Author Statement

Sometimes my experience of writing poetry is like divining for water or prospecting for gold. I let the images bend in the direction of the source of deeper wisdom, and I follow the veins of words to the streams of spirit and the gold of soul.

Other times, writing poetry is like dumpster-diving. The words and images burrow through trash and refuse, trying to get at what lies under all the smelly anxiety and disturbances that keep me from feeling well in myself. I write until I reach a still point, where I can rest. I pause, and look around, and read the poem, and realize I have come to a freer, truer understanding.

I never start with a plan. I am moved by uneasiness or beauty or an image that calls me to stop and notice, and to trust that if I linger in this place of unknowing, I will find meaning. The images call me like small birds, flying from tree to tree. I catch a flash of insight, or a crest of awe, and I write.

The birds that fly from branch to branch with words in their beaks are the same birds that fluttered in my soul with a call: Follow me. Like the dove leaving the ark after the great flood (of Noah's time), I trusted the peace and new world that awaited when I left my vocation of teaching and answered a call to serve in ministry in the United Church of Canada. It was a great joy to apprentice myself to the words of inspiration and mystery that have accompanied poets and artists across time. Now retired from parish ministry, I find myself as a diviner again, in my work as a spiritual director.

It has been several years since my two books were published by Borealis Press: *Rough Angel/ Ange Ecru* (2006, translated into French by Michel Gadoury), and *Spirit Song in Ancient Boughs*. (2008) I had been dancing around the nudge to publish another book of poetry, when the **Don Gutteridge Poetry Prize** inspired me to take the next step and curate my poems into this book, *On Small Wings*. I am thrilled to be included as an inaugural prizewinner. As I was curating my poems, I was surprised to see how many included the images of birds and wings and flight.

I find solace and comfort in the "thin space" where our consciousness blurs into the wider, older, perennial wisdom at the heart of all life. Underneath all our human limitations, the spirit that dwells in all creation offers rest for the soul. Writing poetry connects me (or re-connects me) with this place of wonder, beauty and love. My mother would often refer to me as her "dream-led daughter."

In the last years of her life, as my mother's personality and perspectives were being distorted and diminished by dementia, I sought refuge in the universal mysteries of life and death. As the rituals of her day revolved around her increasing pain and the heart-breaking loss of agency, the smallest moments became sacred: brushing her hair, holding her hand, singing her the songs she taught us as children. She would not recognize herself in the poems I wrote during these times, but she would recognize me, and I hope she would smile.

Sages remind us that the most particular of our experiences are also the most universal. I look to the ancient rhythms of earth and space to teach me, and to share the beauty of each small moment, as it flies, from my heart to yours, on small wings.

Acknowledgements

On Small Wings: previously shared on CASA website (FACEBOOK)
Too Shy to Ask: commissioned by the Vancouver Men's Choir
Friends of Ditches: previously shared on CASA website (FACEBOOK)
When the Robins Come: First Prize in William Henry Drummond contest 2017 (published in Chapbook anthology)

I also would like to extend my gratitude for the generous legacy provided by Donald Gutteridge, and to thank him for the honour of being one of the prize winners in the inaugural Don Gutteridge Poetry Award.

Author Bio Note

Wendy Jean MacLean's everyday life is rimed with numinous light.

Her award-winning poetry explores the untold stories of ordinary objects like buttons and stones, and our deepest humanity. Her work is shaped by a lifelong engagement with mythology, gospel and literature. Published in *Crosswinds, Gathering, Green Spirit, Ancient Paths, CASA, Boosey and Hawkes, GIA, Streetlight, Arborealis. Sheila-na-Gig, Collegeville Bearings Online,* and commissioned and sung internationally. Awards include: the Don Gutteridge Inaugural Poetry Prize; Big Pond Rumours Chapbook; Open Heart; Poetry Matters; the Drummond. Wendy is a retired minister of the United Church and a Spiritual Director.